To all those who have generously allowed their faces
and their stories to appear in this book

Twice in a lifetime | *half lives in camera*

To Mum and Dad – my "fifteen minutes of fame"!
With love from Richard
Christmas 1998

Mark Eban

Twice in a lifetime | *half lives in camera*

Mark Eban

z

zelda cheatle press

First published by zelda cheatle press 1998

99 Mount Street, London W1Y 5HF

0171-408 4448

©Mark Eban 1998

ISBN 1 899823 06 9

All rights are reserved.

No part of this publication may be reproduced or transmitted
in any form or by any means, electronic or mechanical, including
photocopying, recording or any information storage
or retrieval system, without permission from the publishers.

The right of Mark Eban to be identified as author of this work
has been asserted by him in accordance with the
Copyright, Design and Patents Act 1988

British Library Cataloguing in Publication Data.

A catalogue record for this book is available from the British Library.

Designed by Peter Campbell

Printed by BAS Printers

Distributed by Art Books International

Preface

We can tell from appearance the work someone does or does not do; we can read in his face whether he is happy or troubled, for life unavoidably leaves its trace there. A well-known poem says that every person's story is written plainly on his face, though not everyone can read it. These are runes of a new, but also ancient, language...

August Sander, *The Nature and Development of Photography*, Lecture 5, 1931

At Cambridge I took pictures all the time, from arriving at Trinity in 1978 until I graduated in 1981. Looking back through my old contact sheets it seems that I had an obsessive interest in recording the experience. The photographs were, with a few exceptions, taken within Trinity – in undergraduates' rooms, in courtyards, libraries, gardens, the college bar, at parties and on the Backs. Those who appear in this book include friends, acquaintances and strangers. My memories of Cambridge are now shaped by photographs: I have very clear recollections of the circumstances in which each was taken, to such an extent that it seems that whatever is not recorded in one or other of the pictures from that time may never have happened.

After Cambridge I turned to landscape photography. With the exception of my children, people generally seemed less prepared to be photographed casually and in any circumstances.

I had often wondered where life had taken those whom I had photographed at Cambridge. Recent events in my own life had made me realise that if I did not make the effort to find them now, the chance might pass me by. By coincidence, in the same year I had a few months free between jobs in banking and therefore decided to spend that time finding and photographing again as many as I could. I have been lucky in that fifty-five were willing to have their portraits published alongside those of their younger selves, and to write down their own reflections on the years which have passed.

In this process, I have seen striking differences in the lives which had to some extent a common beginning at Cambridge. On one day I travelled from the comfortable surroundings of the Fellows' lunch at an Oxbridge college to a council block where a modern portcullis covered the door. On another I saw a house with startling works of art and one with bare walls. Another day, another journey: from a house dominated by children to one in which they would have seemed quite out of place even as visitors.

The City (particularly of the 1980s) has had a distinct influence. When I left Trinity in 1981, we would have been shocked at the eventual contrast in income between those who drifted into financial services or the legal infrastructure which serves them and those who pursued vocations in the arts, journalism, science, medicine, academia, or the Bar.

There were also patterns. One that I had not noticed before, I saw again and again. The generation of women who were the first to go up to Trinity had succeeded extraordinarily in breaking into traditional male institutions. At the same time they had had to compromise for families and children in a way that the men who were undergraduates with them had not. That early confident equality and comradeship as we remade the world late at night had fallen away. The male role was generally that of the establishment, many womens' careers having been truncated. I sometimes wondered to what extent we had been party to a betrayal.

Despite whatever people have written to accompany their photographs, in conversation many of them echoed my own thoughts: that the life we have now is the result of drift and a few, perhaps random, decisions. Many of us are now reconsidering past definitions of success. Perhaps in twenty years I will do this again and see if anyone has found any answers.

Mark Eban
September 1998

Twice in a lifetime

Neil Adams. I look rather innocent and naïve in the photograph, which is what I probably was. I find it surprising now to realise how little I thought about the future then. At the time I focussed on the Maths, which was time-consuming but fun, and did not really do an awful lot socially, which I now regret. I enjoyed university up to a point, but must say that after eight years there (degree plus one year study plus PhD) I had had enough of

academia – I wanted to get out into the real world where one could (I believed) do work with an end in mind, not just for the sake of advancing knowledge. On the whole I have been able to do that. I have worked in jobs that have mostly been related to supporting the RAF, either in sorting out current problems with aircraft and systems or looking at what equipment they will need twenty years from now. Cambridge now seems a bit

like a museum to me: a place I visit on rare occasions but not a place to which I pay much attention.

On the personal level I would like to think life will carry on much as now, that I will continue to work as a government scientist worrying about protecting the country from all threats. Once you get bitten by the public service bug you find the concept of working simply to earn a profit for a company and yourself rather

barren. Also, working with service personnel who train for war, fight, and on occasion die has given me a rather different perspective from the average nine-to-five job. However I suspect this is not going to happen. It may be that the contracting civil service will make me go in a new career direction, although into what I am not sure. Alternatively more significant events may change things for my family and many others in ways I can only barely imagine. Twenty years ago I did not really think much about the future, but ended up doing the sort of job (government scientist) and marrying the sort of girl (another government scientist) I would have expected. Now I do think a lot about the future but the error bars on what might happen are so large I know that predicting what the future might hold is not sensible.

Matriculated: 1976. *Graduated:* 1979. *Studied:* Mathematics. *Left Trinity:* 1984 (PhD in Applied Mathematics – Black Holes). *Family:* Married with three-year-old daughter. *Lives in:* Bracknell, Berkshire. *Works as:* Civil servant, Defence Evaluation and Research Agency. *Car:* I have just traded in my first car (a fifteen year old Volvo 340GL) for a Nissan Primera (for the reliability and air conditioning). *Income:* not disclosed

Richard Bailey. Looking at this picture I know exactly when it was taken for the simple reason that my desk was only once this tidy. I had rearranged my furniture, probably the day before and had yet to discover that, when not up against a wall, paper fell off the back of the desk and was much more difficult to sort through! What really surprises me is the total absence of electronic media beyond a pocket calculator. I understand that today all college rooms are networked using fibre-optics and can't imagine students not having some sort of computer. I shouldn't think any are equipped with no less than three bottles of Quink – was I really that verbose? I know I'm still using the same fountain pen, partly because it's comfortable for my 'RSI' like symptoms that are one result of twenty years technical computing.

Do I recognise the person looking out of the picture? Yes and I think that he would recognise me – someone still focussed on finding the 'right' answer to technical problems, still a little apprehensive about softer issues and reluctant to trust intuition when challenged to come to swift decisions, in other words characteristics of the engineering and scientific disciplines. Really Cambridge gave me the confidence to express ideas and investigate phenomena mathematic-

ally leading to a career in Engineering Consultancy. It also led directly to my meeting my wife!

Since then a short biography might identify only two key decisions: the first being marriage and the second not to take a company move to Scotland. No regrets to date, or anticipated, about either. The next twenty years? – completely unpredictable. After all, did that twenty-year-old undergraduate expect to give lifts to hitch-hiking Botswanian policemen, look down the wrong end of an AK47 held by a barefoot Government soldier, travel to work in the Colombian Andes by helicopter or dodge caribou in Alaska? The answer is most definitely not – life is what you make it, but also what it offers you!

Matriculated: 1978. *Graduated:* 1982. *Studied:* Chemical Engineering (via Natural Sciences). *Lives in:* Ashtead, Surrey. *Works as:* Chartered Chemical Engineer. *Family:* Wife, Anne (Girton, graduated 1982, Classics); Alexander James (7 years), William Stephen (5 years), No. 3 anticipated March 1999. *Cars:* P-reg. Volvo V70 2.5, D-reg. MG Maestro, V-reg. MG Midget. *Income:* upper quartile according to professional institution surveys

Gawain Barnard. I like to try and think exclusively about the future and leave much of what is past un-remembered; so I'm not surprised I had forgotten about the central baths then used at Trinity or the instant of this photograph. Though the memories of the pain, and strangely the smell, of the Cambridge University Amateur Boxing Club training sessions remain.

Of the constants that I've chosen to include in my own half-life, physical competition still ranks highly. Through this I have encountered many fascinating places and people.

I have lived in Europe and the Middle East over the last few years, but write this on a Bloomberg screen in Tokyo, which is

where I plan to be based for as long as I can reasonably plan ahead (sometime pretty early in the next millennium).

I am travelling light in life at the moment, though ideally won't always do so. I am looking forward to picking the next thing to work towards from the varied balance I am fortunate enough to have in front of me.

Matriculated: 1978. Graduated: 1982. *Studied:* History Part I, Arabic Part I. *Lives in:* Tokyo. *Works as:* Investment banker (sales). *Family:* Divorced, no children. *Car:* Aprillia motor bike. *Income:* not disclosed

Heidi Bartlet. When I saw my old photo I thought, 'Trinity Bar seems an appropriate setting'. Before I went to Cambridge it stood for a place to fulfil my academic aspirations, but looking back it was certainly the social aspect that had the most impact. And I discovered I wouldn't have a future as a theoretical physicist. I have kept up with just a couple of friends from Trinity but find it is always interesting to hear snippets of gossip about others I knew – Mark has gathered some interesting and surprising facts.

When I left Cambridge I had no idea of what direction my life would take. I knew I wanted a break from anything too academic or pressurised and I didn't want to get slotted into a career which I might not escape!

I filled my time working with children with learning disabilities, travelling overseas, helping squat a redundant UB40 building (re-christened 'The Pig and Bailiff'), visiting Greenham Common and generally indulging in an Exeter-style Anarcho-Hippy way of life.

By the age of twenty-nine I had eventually reached the point where I thought perhaps I was ready for a career and trained as an occupational therapist. Since then I have worked with children and with adults and am currently working in the psychiatric services for the over 65s.

My life has taken on a whole new dimension since meeting Peter three years ago and the birth of our daughter Holly just over a year ago. It does surprise me at times that I have become – to a greater extent than I would ever have expected – a housewife! However life with the two of them is excellent and I now work for three days a week and greatly enjoy my long weekends.

Matriculated: 1978. *Graduated:* 1981. *Studied:* Experimental Psychology. *Lives in:* Hilton, Cambridgeshire (a village 12 miles from Cambridge with 800 residents, 80 ducks and a Turf Maze). *Works as:* Occupational therapist for the National Health Service. *Family:* Peter (partner) and Holly (15 months). *Car:* Renault Clio. *Income:* £19,000 pro rata

Dave Beadle. Since Trinity I've been a van-driver and worked for research, TV, consultancy, and advertising companies/agencies – so I'm still playing with ideas and talking bollocks. I'm also still going to gigs, seeing the dawn in with friends, and cleaning the stains from the bean-bag. And dope's still £15 a quarter. At present I'm spending a redundancy cheque, so maybe now's the time to finish that screenplay…

The moustache came off on my thirty-fifth birthday to maintain my youthful good looks, so please ignore the photos.

My partner Anne, though, gets better-looking each year. We met outside Tesco's rattling buckets for the Miners. After that we launched Enfield's Anti-Apartheid group (responding to BNP threats the only way they respect), I've been illegally arrested at Wapping, done my stint as an Enfield councillor (the only one prosecuted for non-payment of the Poll Tax) etc, etc. I draw the line at public school Oxbridge graduates going to Parliament to represent working-class people. Unimpressed with my Linkline

nights at Cambridge, however, the Samaritans asked me to go away.

My son Chris goes to a multi-cultural, mixed-sex, no-uniform state school. Nine years old and 4 foot 10 inches, he doesn't pick fights or get picked on, but does stand up for his mates. He's only been arrested once.

Serendipity continues to deliver new discoveries, and life's cooool.

Matriculated: 1977. *Graduated:* 1980. *Studied:* Economics (sometimes, really). *Lives in:* Bounds Green, North London. *Works as:* 'Consultant' (middle-class jobbing labour). *Family:* Anne (partner), Christopher (son), Taxi (cat). *Family (extended):* Tony (Irish republican neighbour), Doris (octogenarian neighbour), Shirley, Peter (mum, dad), Paddy (their dog), Claire, Nick, Leah, Sacha (sister, brother-in-law, nieces), Trevor, Julie, Tom, Ollie (brother, sister-in-law, nephews), Simon (Chelsea fan), Vicky (German friend). *Union:* GMB. *Car:* J-reg. Cavalier (with 50,000 taken off the clock to maintain its youth...). *Income:* £70 an hour (but for you...)

Rachel Bell. I was 18 when I went up to Cambridge.

I remember waking up on the first day at Trinity and thinking: Oh God, I'm never going to be able to go home again; from now on I've got to make my own home because that's what you have to do when you are a grown-up.

Like everyone, probably, I often felt less successful, less glowing, less supremely self-assured than other people.

This picture must have been taken in my first term: seeing it now I was first surprised by how tough I look; then alarmed by my vulnerability. It doesn't make me think 'how little I knew then...' because I never thought it was going to be easy.

What I didn't realise was just how difficult it would be to have the same ambitions as the men I knew while being a woman with a family. I have, of course, made my own home: I have two children whom I adore, a career and lots of friends. Two years ago, my American husband left us. My mother brought me up on two classic middle-class mantras: 'Life isn't fair' and 'Rise above it, darling.' Now I find myself saying both of them with alarming frequency.

Matriculated: 1980. *Graduated:* 1983. *Studied:* History. *Lives in:* Bristol. *Works as:* TV producer, BBC. *Family:* Angus (5 years) and Lily (7 years). *Car:* H-reg. Ford Orion Ghia. *Income:* £40,000

Sarah Brown. I've always admired Mark's first picture – all those rounded shapes. But I've always thought it an odd representation of me, because I think of myself as a spiky person. And here I am round again. The difference between then and now? Then I thought I'd have a Career, in something creative but I wasn't sure what. Then I thought that if I had children I'd take six months off and go back to work. Then I thought adulthood was something I would have achieved by now. Now I look at my life since then and see how very different it has been. I've had jobs, but no career path; I've had children, and then hardly 'worked' for six years. And I still don't feel like an adult. Instead of making some small mark on history, I've done strange and wonderful things I never knew I'd do. I've achieved a lifelong dream and lived in Africa. I've

walked with the Samburu through north-ern Kenya. I've dived to a wreck in clear waters. I've lived on a beach in the Gulf and seen tankers and dhows strung across the offing at sunset. And I've enjoyed staying with my children.

These seem more defining experiences than any of my many jobs. When I look back I realise that I was a jack of all trades at school and at university, so perhaps my eclectic life after Cambridge is not so surprising after all.

Matriculated (Girton): 1980. *Graduated:* 1983. *Studied:* Engineering and Geog-raphy. *Lives in:* Wimbledon, London. *Works as:* Jobs have included costumier, video producer, TV researcher, journalist, foreign correspondent and writer. *Family:* Married to Neil Fleming, three daughters. *Car:* B-reg. bright red Mercedes estate. *Income:* none

Nigel Burney. Mark had a peculiarly sympathetic mien as he showed me his masterpiece of me, captured during the one hour and ten minutes that I spent in the Law Reading Room in three years. If ever a photo defined bewildered panic in the face of imminent and inescapable exam disaster, this was it. My tutor foresaw the danger in my first essay, whose one and a half pages, allegedly wrestling with opening themes of contract law, drew one eloquently brief sentence: 'This is the worst essay I have ever read'.

Cambridge was the first time I had had the awe-inspiring opportunity to interface with real life: for example, deciding the ideal time to surface to face the exigencies of the day was a year-long project in its own right, and was still being regularly reviewed for flaws in year three.

University was as particularly useful for discovering what not to do and how not to do it as it was for the reverse. My main achievement, I think, was in deconstructing prejudices rather than refining them and lasting value came from the friendships made and kept.

Having gone on, in dogged disregard of the tea-leaves, and qualified as a solicitor, I left the law to start a business immediately. Tellingly, my firm had also come to the conclusion that I represented their surest avenue to massive profes-

sional negligence suits, and had taken the precaution at the earliest stage of not offering me further employment either.

The last fifteen years has been spent in starting, growing and, in some case, losing, businesses and has been really exciting and challenging. Work suddenly became a pleasure, an addiction at times, and has pushed me to all ends of the emotional register. The two aspects I have found really brilliant have been the con-

tinual necessity to learn about and direct people and the freedom to take total responsibility for my own destiny. I feel that my most creative years are still ahead.

On the personal side, I met my wife, Lucy, in a late sortie in amateur dramatics. I played her father and, at that stage, she quite rightly rejected my advances with shock and disdain. A rather complicated joke about incest in my wedding speech bombed as well!

We now have two wonderful boys, Max and Otto, who, I think, are bringing us both up rather well. I am really grateful to Mark for doing this project.

Matriculated: 1978. *Graduated:* 1981. *Studied:* Law. *Lives in:* Wandsworth, London. *Works as:* Publishing/Financial Services. *Family:* Wife, Lucy (*née* Brooks), Max (3 years) and Otto (2 years). *Car:* J-reg. Mercedes. *Income:* in a sharp 'up' phase

Paul Chapman. I have some photos from Trinity, too. I lost most of my past traumatically in a car theft in Washington DC in 1983. Letters and diaries and personal mementoes: all went to feed briefly the braziers of the homeless. My negatives were too bulky to take on the trip. Not sure I'd want to add to them now. I'd rather fix those faces in the past, thirsting for experience, than risk finding them careworn in the present day.

I travelled and lived abroad a lot in the early 1980s. After that, I tried a pension plan and mortgage in the suburbs, but found I didn't suit the life. Now I enjoy an untidy, rented flat with a wood-panelled study on a lively street in Bloomsbury. I don't often wander much further than the café opposite, except to visit West End cinemas. I now explore the wider world in cyberspace, where you might stumble upon me writing with equal parts of skill and ignorance on films and every other subject under the sun.

I am disproportionately proud that all four letters I have so far submitted for publication in periodicals have been printed. I sometimes wish that people would only speak publicly when they have something worth saying and can say it well.

I am currently in my tenth year of celibacy. Sex is like punting: you do it regularly for a while, you enjoy it, maybe you're reasonably good at it. Then you move away from the river to a drier environment. Some might say desiccated.

I have a great deal of time for a tiny number of friends, most of them fellow smokers; all of them content not to compete too hard for false glory. I remain passionate about movies, space exploration, cosmology, justice, and the declining quality of grammar in the printed media. I am interested in everything but football, food, finance, family life and folk music, which is to say everything not beginning with f. I am an optimist, and therefore expect that I shall eventually die. I am also an atheist, and therefore trust that that will be an end to it. My favourite colour is grey.

Matriculated: 1976. *Graduated:* 1979. *Studied:* Mathematics and Computer Science. *Lives in:* Bloomsbury, London. *Works as:* Freelance computer programmer. *Family:* Single, no children. *Car:* Not any more. *Income:* just what I need, when I need it

Tim Dawson. I am looking at the picture from nearly twenty years ago. Did we really try so hard to live like extras in *Brideshead Revisited*? I am relieved to be able to say that although I still have my First & Third bow tie, it has not been worn since I left. However, let's not pretend that it wasn't all immensely enjoyable at the time, because it was. Since leaving, the college has not played a big rôle in my life. Most of my friends either pre-date or post-date my time at Trinity. That is down to my laziness and is certainly not a reflection on the people I knew at the time whom I liked and I rather regret allowing to drift away.

Living in London and working in the City is pretty much how I saw my future when I left. As for marriage and children, that was not a question that had even begun to register. Now it seems entirely natural. I suppose looking back the surprise is how relatively easily everything seems to have fallen into place.

Strangely, the work-related future appears more uncertain now than it did when I left Trinity (or maybe it's just that the uncertainty is more deeply felt). The financial markets industry (my area of it, anyway) seems to be dominated by people aged thirty to forty so a significant change seems quite probable. I am very lucky because my wife's profession is one that is also a business so there may be an obvious exit route. Overall, I think I have been very fortunate in the way things have developed and the way choices have turned out, especially given how uninformed I feel I was when I made those choices, or at least the ones about work.

Matriculated: 1978. *Graduated:* 1981. *Studied:* Mathematics. *Lives in:* Wandsworth, London. *Works as:* Investment analyst. *Family:* Wife, Cressida, dentist; 2 boys Jeanot (5 years), Fitzwilliam (4 years). *Cars:* M-reg. Mercedes SL, K-reg. Mercedes Estate. *Income:* not disclosed

Adam de Courcy Ling, Chris Fordham

Adam de Courcy Ling. My main impression on seeing this old picture was that I clearly wasn't supposed to be there, being the head accidentally in the foreground of someone else's portrait shot. Mark assures me he didn't just drop the camera as Chris Fordham went by.

When this shot was taken, I think shortly after my matriculation in 1979, I was studying history and aspiring to a brief and prosperous business career followed by a glorious political one.

Having eschewed the milk round as a matter of principle, I went off in 1982 to Munich to work for Albrecht Matuschka, an eccentric German banker in whose employment I thought fame and fortune could be gained more rapidly and painlessly (and my German would improve more) than in traditional professional training in London. The choice also just seemed more fun, while I furthermore naïvely (and wrongly) imagined that, after three years indolence at Cambridge, the Germans would also teach me how to work. Although indolence proved indelible, the connection with Germany has turned out to be a career and I am now, sixteen years later, responsible for mergers and acquisitions in Germany at Credit Suisse First Boston, the Swiss/ American investment bank. The attraction to politics has wilted, at least for the time being.

In 1992, I re-met and in 1995 married Clare Pearson, who read history at Jesus a year behind me and, in addition to all her other contributions, also provides the academic distinction in my life. The smaller person in the newer photo is our daughter, Harriet, born in January 1996, who holds her father in adoring subjugation all day. Clare refused to appear on the grounds that she was too heavily pregnant. Mark was born in June 1998.

We distinguished him from Mark Eban by giving him 'Francis' rather than 'Eban' as a second name. We live next to Chelsea Barracks in London.

Early morning flights to Frankfurt and the rigours of small children weren't at the top of the list of my aspirations at the time the original photograph was taken. While the second isn't such a surprise, it continues to astonish me that I've now made a career of flying to Germany. I

rationalise it to myself that, as the son of a diplomat, I must have a genetic need for the illusory glamour of foreign languages, strange customs and those early morning flights.

Matriculated; 1979. *Graduated:* 1982. *Studied:* History. *Lives in:* Chelsea, London. *Works as:* Investment banker. *Family:* Wife, Clare; daughter, Harriet (nearly 3 years old), son Mark (June 1998). *Car:* Volkswagen Golf. *Income:* not disclosed

Chris Fordham. What did I think when I saw the old picture? I thought, 'Those poor dons. Those poor dons who had to teach us, arrogant and ignorant students, and read our essays, and lecture us, and listen to our silly views, and pretend to take them seriously and encourage us to be creative and work harder, and not rage at our ignorance and our stupidity. And the worst of it? Many of them must still be doing the same, but with Cambridge students who are thicker still, and idler, uglier and duller than we were. Those poor dons. Poor Cambridge.'

Fifteen 'choices' since leaving Cambridge (in chronological order):

1. To keep my Cambridge friends

2. To throw away my favourite Trinity stripy trousers

3. To find a job

4. To bemoan the loss of the Gardenia and the old Cambridge market which sold vegetables, not 'snow storms'

5. To take a masters degree

6. To marry a beautiful and successful Finn

7. To get a proper job, and enjoy it

8. To be a bore about Cambridge days

9. To have a haircut

10. To have three babes, all more beautiful than me

11. To believe that today's Cambridge students are thicker, idler, uglier, duller than we were

12. To grow grey hair

13. To master the Finnish language

14. To avoid becoming a management consultant

15. To smile about all things except the loss of my favourite Trinity stripy trousers

And the next twenty years? In the next twenty years, I hope to be wealthy enough to commission some new stripy trousers.

Matriculated: 1979. *Graduated:* 1982. *Studied:* History. *Lives in:* Notting Hill, London. *Works as:* Marketing director Haymarket Publishing. *Family:* Wife, Sally; two daughters, Lucca and Cazalla, and one son, Alexander. *Car:* L-reg. Shogun. *Income:* not disclosed

Helena Drysdale. Young free and single... That's what this photo made me think, with a twinge of nostalgia. I loved Cambridge. I loved the frivolity, and my independence. I also loved the place. I suffered from anorexic insecurities, but at least I had a beautiful backdrop. London seems brutal in comparison.

When I left Cambridge I was bored with parties, and set off on an exciting but sometimes lonely path. While preparing my Cambridge dissertation I had decided to be a writer. I began as an art critic, then worked for a newspaper. But I was frustrated with writing about other peoples' lives, and not living myself. So after ten months I left, and went to India.

Alone in the Himalayas, I came wonderfully alive. I wrote my first book, and have been travelling and writing ever since. Fortunately I married a like-minded man. We've just spent two years on the road with our daughters, researching a book about Europe.

Richard and I didn't really decide to get married, it just seemed obvious. We married four months after we met, and that was eleven years ago.

My life is perhaps more isolated than I'd envisaged. Richard and I both work at home, sharing the childcare. I often dream of putting on tights, striding off to some office, and rejoining the world, but then I look at my daughters and know I couldn't leave them, or forsake what's left of my freedom. It may happen in the next twenty years; it's something I'm going to have to get out of my system.

Matriculated: 1978. *Graduated:* 1982. *Studied:* History Part I, History of Art Part II. *Lives in:* Stockwell, London. *Works as:* Writer. *Family:* Husband, Richard Pomeroy (photographer and painter); daughters Tallulah (5 years) and Xanthe (2 years). *Car:* White. *Income:* sporadic

Mark Eban. I was only sixteen when I took my A-levels; so even after Cambridge Entrance and a year off, I was only seventeen when I went up. Cambridge was therefore perhaps even more of a revelation for me than it was for some of my contemporaries. I loved every moment of it, the new freedom, the new emotions, the new traumas, and I felt driven to try to capture as much of it as possible in my photography. I am also sure that giving myself the tools of an observer helped me cope with my own limited social skills.

This original picture is relevant to me for a number of reasons: it reminds me how young I looked; it reminds me of the sense of proprietorship I had over my Great Court room; and the camera I am holding reminds me of the injustice I have done to myself (and I am sure others) by the brash and arrogant attitude that came with getting into Cambridge so early. You see it wasn't my camera. It was an extremely valuable Leica with an ultra fast lens. It was lent to me by one of the Fellows for a couple of weeks. Because I had never really worked at anything (not

for A-levels, not for Cambridge Entrance and certainly not during my time at Cambridge) I only understood the easy route. I didn't understand how to learn or listen. Even at the time the design of the camera was old-fashioned and the lens produced images of an unusual quality (several are in this book). It was a craftsman's camera and despite photography

being my passion I couldn't make the effort to learn the craft. I stayed like that for a long time, most especially in my emotional relationships.

Today, I feel unfrozen in time: that I can learn from other people; that 'winning' is not so important; that one can be happy in the present and that having children has made me a much kinder person.

Matriculated: 1978. *Graduated:* 1981. *Studied:* Law. *Lives in:* St. Johns Wood, London and Rookley, Isle of Wight. *Works as:* Investment banker. *Family:* Wife, Anna Guggenheim; Edward (6 years) and Rachel (4 years). *Car:* L-reg. Volvo 940 Estate. *Income:* not as much as a number of people I know which used to make me miserable but now doesn't (much)

John Elmes. The old photo was the first 'mug shot' I used to send out to theatres and agents to try to get work. Looking at it now, I'm not at all surprised that I played a lot of schoolboys at the start of my career. My face then seems very young and naïve (and spotty) now.

I got into Cambridge by following the path of least resistance, because I didn't have a clue about what I actually wanted to do. I only read Engineering because it was the most obvious choice for someone who was good at passing exams in Maths, Physics and Chemistry.

It was the prospect of the party that was Cambridge ending at graduation, and wanting to carry on being happy that forced me to make a Decision. That's how I set off on the journey that led me to the second photo. If I'd stayed an engineer I'd probably be richer, I would have worked more regularly, and I'd certainly have a better pension. But then I'd never have met my wonderful wife, and we'd

never have had our two beautiful children. I'd never have played a Victorian melodrama in a packed tent in wildest Cumbria, filmed on Exmoor with Virginia McKenna and a herd of llamas, spent months on end without any prospect of work, heard the moment of silence before the applause at the end of an all-day trilogy of plays about the war in Northern Ireland, lived without any financial security, ordered a drink in the Rovers Return, and I wouldn't be writing this in my dressing room in the West End doing Shaw and Molière eight times a week. There are things I regret, but that Decision isn't one of them.

Matriculated: 1978. *Graduated:* 1981. *Studied:* Engineering. *Lives in:* Camberwell, London. *Works as:* Actor. *Family:* Married with two children. *Car:* Yes. *Income:* irregular

Ermine Evans. I just thought how sweet I looked in some of the photos Mark showed me. In this photo I look rather serious. I met Richard, on my left, in my first year but we didn't go out until our third year when this picture was taken. He was an architecture student and went to Hong Kong in my fourth year. And he married the nanny he met there. No accounting for taste.

I didn't make long-term plans then. I guess if you'd asked me I'd have said I'd be married with 2.4 kids, a Labrador and a Volvo by now. I had the Volvo in my last job - but somehow the kids and husband haven't materialised!

After Cambridge, I went into the City, which I enjoyed but wasn't enthralled by the idea of doing the same thing in ten year's time. So I went to business school

without a clear idea about my next move.

After INSEAD I had just started working for the Chairman and Chief Executive of an engineering company in Birmingham when he died. My rôle was made redundant, which was a very hard knock, because it was the first job that had really motivated me. I suppose it was also the first real adversity I'd known. In 1992, I applied for a job running enter-

prise programmes in Eastern Europe. They offered me a job in the Finance Division of the Department of Transport, which I took. It was a fascinating three years and I learnt that you don't have to be able to do sums to manage £1 billion.

I went to Surrey in 1995 to set up and run the Business Link. I learnt a lot there and am now a good general manager. I'm proud of the team and the results we achieved. I was headhunted in the summer to work at Business Link London City Partners so am now back in my old stamping ground, the City.

Life is becoming better and better. I love living in London and being with my friends and family. My career will continue to develop in the interface between the private and public sectors. I will also develop my interest in neuro-linguistics and coaching. I'm much more focused now and have some clear goals.

Matriculated: 1978. *Graduated:* 1982. *Studied:* Law Part I, Social & Political Science Part II. *Lives in:* Pimlico, London. *Works as:* Chief Executive of Business Link London City Partners (from November 1998). *Family:* Single, no children. *Car:* None – still got a pushbike! *Income:* small relative to yours, Mark!

Emma Fearnhamm. Emma declined to
write a piece for this book.
 *Matriculated: 1980. Graduated: 1983.
Studied: History. Lives in: East End of
London. Works as: School-teacher. Family:*
Single, no children

Fabian French. Looking at Mark's pictures of me, I barely recognise myself. I look incredibly young, naïve and rather vulnerable – which I suppose I was. I think I was very immature and insecure and the biggest change in the last twenty years is probably a much higher degree of self-confidence.

My nutshell recollection of Trinity is:

Year 1 – one long party, revelling in a new-found freedom, making new friends and doing no work.

Year 2 – realising I won't get a degree if I don't do some work, feeling guilty about partying so much, discovering that most of my new 'friends' aren't.

Year 3 – living out and spending hours on a bicycle, discovering where the law library is and finding a balance between fun and work.

By far the most significant event took place on the first day of my first term at Trinity: I met my future wife. We didn't start going out until 1987 and were married in 1990, but our *When Harry met Sally* relationship began that day. So really Trinity was more a successful dating agency for me than a seat of learning.

I became a solicitor after Cambridge because I was too scared of earning

nothing at the Bar for years. I then went into investment banking, which I have greatly enjoyed. It is a demanding environment in which to work, but being a naturally lazy person I need the adrenaline to keep me going. It also happens to pay rather well, which is good because both Pippa and I have expensive tastes.

Have I taken a major career decision or risks? No, not really, but I have already decided when I am going to leave the City and what I'm going to do afterwards, which will be something quite different.

Most significant event: becoming a father. It has created a whole new set of priorities, challenges and objectives. Having three healthy, charming and intelligent children is a huge privilege and has made me much more conscious of divine involvement in our lives.

Matriculated: 1978. *Graduated:* 1981. *Studied:* Modern Languages Part I and Law Part II. *Lives in:* Notting Hill, London. *Works as:* Investment banker. *Family:* Wife, Pippa (Trinity 1978-1981); 6-year-old triplets, Hugo, Olivia and Rosie. *Cars:* Mercedes Estate, Land Rover Discovery and 1972 Triumph TR6. *Income:* not disclosed

Pippa Latham. At Cambridge, it took me most of the three years to find my feet as I was shy and unsophisticated. As you can see from my picture I used to hide in the library! But I have never looked back and always go for the challenges. Despite the spirit of competitiveness, which had driven me to get into Trinity, I always thought I would marry a rich farmer and bring up a family in rural comfort.

But the driving spirit has always been dominant and with a bit of subtle paternal guidance I followed a commercial route from economics through merchant bank-ing into industry, picking up an MBA and a couple of professional qualifications on the way. Eight years later I still work in the family timber-importing business and combine this with a happy family life married to the wonderful Fabian and mother to the six-year-old 'Fabian look-

alikes' Olivia, Rosie and Hugo. We live in London and dream of rural sunrises, heavy dew on the lawn and red kites circling overhead. One day! In the meantime, I might do a PhD part-time and make sure that I spend positive, fun time with the children adopting the Suzuki philosophy in life as well as with music (Hugo and Rosie learn the violin and Olivia the piano).

Matriculated: 1978. *Graduated:* 1981. *Studied:* Economics. *Lives in:* Notting Hill, London. *Works as:* Company Secretary, family timber-importing business. *Family:* Husband, Fabian (Trinity 1978-1981); 6-year-old triplets, Hugo, Olivia and Rosie. *Income:* not disclosed

Ralph Godsall. I returned to Cambridge as Chaplain of Trinity College at the beginning of the Michaelmas Term 1978 and remained in post until the summer of 1984.

Twenty years on – and somewhat greyer – I have much the same appetite for religion (provided it is not too narrow and eclectic). I remain content with the Church of England and am glad to be in parish ministry in central London. I maintain my love of the outdoors and am gradually climbing all the Scottish Munros (155 out of 284 notched up already)! I didn't know what to expect after my years at Trinity, but do remember (with affection) that Bishop John Robinson, the Dean of Chapel, hoped

that my years as a college chaplain would prepare me for active ministry in several key parishes. I'm doing that just now and from this central position find myself bumping into more and more former undergraduates in the City and in the bars and restaurants of nearby Pimlico!

I ride a bicycle most of the time. When I have to get in a car, I drive a VW Passat Estate.

The parish provides me with an ample town house in Vincent Square, London, and the Church Commissioners ensure that I receive an annual stipend of £14,900! How I miss Trinity's very generous 'entertainment allowance' for the chaplains!

Giles Goodfellow. Looking at the photograph, I can easily detect in the subject a burning ambition to be a portly barrister, living in Wandsworth driving a Volvo – which is probably just as well. The demon drink continues to play a significant, if more benign, rôle: I met my wife at the tenth Anniversary Ball of the Campaign for Real Gin. Life in the

Zimmer lane is surprisingly fast and fun, with three young boys and a lovely wife keeping me up to the mark.

Long may it continue!
Matriculated: 1979. *Graduated:* 1982. *Studied:* Law. *Lives in:* Wandsworth,

London. *Works as:* Tax barrister. *Family:* Wife and three sons. *Car:* Volvo. *Income:* not disclosed

Richard Harman. Parties on the backs, in each others' rooms, at Adrian Poole's house. Time spent in pursuit of pleasure and distraction and sometimes connection, and I suppose in pursuit of self. A pretty undirected, chaotic, hedonistic time, really, when seen in the rear view-mirror. I suppose I must have done some work as well, at some point.

Last year I went through a period of re-evaluation when I decided that it had been a mistake to go to Cambridge and study English at all. I had not really made any positive choices and I had been drifting down that path with no clarity of purpose. I still think that there is some truth in that observation, though it is more simply expressed as the idea that I really should be going to university now, as I approach forty, and that this would in general be a better way to structure our working and

studying lives. Otherwise, so much time and so many resources are wasted.

The biggest changes since I graduated have been to do with my faith, my family, and my career. None of these were predictable in 1981, at least not to me. Through all of them, however, I have the sense that, out of chaos and uncertainty twenty years ago, some kind of shape and meaning is beginning to emerge, even though I can only vaguely see its outline from time to time.

Matriculated: 1978. *Graduated*: 1981. *Studied*: English Literature. *Lives in*: Eastbourne, East Sussex. *Works as*: Registrar, Eastbourne College. *Family*: Wife, Dr. Karin Voth Harman; one daughter, Olivia (6 years). *Car*: K-reg. Ford Escort Estate. *Income*: mid £30,000s

David Henshaw. I recall Mark showing me my old picture a few weeks ago. I'm looking (slightly heavy-lidded) into the camera, a serious (not to say deep and meaningful) expression, seated at my desk (an implicit reference to study and learning), in a zip-up jumper (an implicit reference to sartorial failure) and I realise just how far away those Cambridge days are. The camera cannot lie (I'm saying nothing about the photographer). I remember thinking how lucky I was and that undergraduate days were the best of one's life. I say this only to point out that happiness, a key component of my memories, is not recorded strongly here in the silver bromide.

In fact I would say that I enjoyed my post-graduate life even more than my undergraduate life (even though it was at the other place) for two reasons. Firstly it was for fifty-two weeks a year (rather than three eight-week bursts) and thus was a better introduction to independence and maturity. Secondly I was a large fish in a small pool (becoming President of St. John's MCR) as opposed to a small fish in a big pool (becoming the bloke in the zip-up jumper).

But life moves on ... and with it come new challenges. Some old challenges still remain of course, such as wondering how serious to look when Mark is taking a

photo, but growing with a family, coping with problems at work, developing my singing in local opera … all bring satisfying rewards.

Did I expect to be here now? Yes and no – on the one hand my career progression has been late starting (!), whereas in leisure I've achieved more in singing than I dreamed of, and (although I imagined a perfect family in the rare moments one considers it) in my wife and my 0.4 children below average I consider myself lucky.

Where will I be in twenty years time? Well …I expect to have progressed further at work (i.e. I don't learn from experience) than in singing (musical careers being precarious) and be preparing to pay for two family weddings. I'm fairly laid-back in the balance between contentment and ambition.

We'll see.

Matriculated: 1978. Graduated: 1981.

Studied: Natural Sciences. *Lives in:* Melbourne (rural town), Derbyshire. *Works as:* Project engineer, Rolls-Royce plc (Aero-Engines, not the cars), Derby. *Family:* Wife (St. Hilda's Oxford) Classics Teacher, Loughborough High School; two daughters Emma (7 years) and Rebecca (4 years). *Car:* Rover 216SLi (regrets cabriolet became impractical with child-related chattels). *Income:* insufficient

Louise Ireland. We spent no time at all considering how we would manage looking after our children and earning a living, we just did it. And it is nice. Very nice. I work part-time, Peter works part-time and the boys – Jack, five, and William, two – have one or other of us all the time. Friends think of us as either brave or barmy. What we are mainly is happy and tired. Peter used to bring Jack and William to St Brides in Fleet Street, just by the Reuters office, for 'milk breaks' when

they were very little and only consuming
breast milk. We had lovely organ music
but the pews were a little uncomfortable.
   Matriculated: 1979. Graduated: 1982.

Studied: English. *Lives in:* Battersea,
London. *Works as:* Journalist. *Family:* Peter
(partner) and two sons. *Car:* Yes. *Income:*
not disclosed

Saul Jacka. The first two years at Cambridge were something of a disappointment. I suppose I was young and spoilt but I was surprised how hard it was to find people who realised that thinking is fun but that one does not live solely to think. Life got better thereafter as I began to meet other people who sought a middle ground between the hearties and the aesthetes. I went to Trinity because I was told that every budding mathematician should seek to do so: in retrospect I think the education was, in the main, mediocre, but I did acquire some pointers as to how to be myself rather than seeking to be all things to all men.

Life since Cambridge has, generally, been on an upward trend. A few good friends including my wife are some of the happy relics of that time, while living a life not centred around the acquisition of money has been a good move. I've stuck to the middle ground by becoming an academic mathematician whilst keeping

a few farm animals – it's hard to be an aesthete standing in cow-muck.

My biggest regrets are not personal – they relate to the way our generation and the one before have failed the coming one. When I talk to my students their lives seem so purposeful yet empty, and I have serious worries about the number who have started considering their pension arrangements. We attempt to redress the balance with our own, much-loved, daughters, and we have all taken up a martial art in the hope that it will give them a chance at a more self-reliant and exciting adolescence than most I see.

Matriculated: 1976. *Graduated:* 1979. *Studied:* Mathematics. *Left Trinity:* 1983. *Lives in:* Bishampton, Worcestershire. *Works as:* Academic (Reader in statistics at Warwick University). *Family:* Wife and two daughters. *Car:* Volkswagen Golf Estate. *Income:* c. £45,000 including consulting and editorships

Vanessa Mackworth-Praed. Despite the fact that my family has gone to Trinity for generations, I felt so lucky to get there and I have never stopped feeling un-nervingly lucky ever since. I was a nervous wreck then and twenty years and count-less yoga sessions have changed nothing.

I pleaded in 1982 to work as a serf in a stockbroking dealing room, adding up columns of figures for six months. By the end of two weeks I could make the same figure come out at the bottom twice in a row, and I was promoted. As with all good novels, characters have reappeared in life to help me along and pay my wages, and after four years of 'proper' work, and five years as a country stock-broker, letting old ladies spend some of their money on fixing the leaks in their roofs, I retired.

Since then I have looked after two exultant children, two ebullient dogs, two under-confident ponies, one stroppy cow, five indolent sheep and, occasionally, an

increasingly hard-working husband.

A part of me feels that I should put all that education and experience to use to earn a decent living again, but then you only get one life and having always lived like a student, perhaps I don't know what I am missing.

I think I am now much more interested in how things work, from water-mills to geological formations, and I have mucked about with a lot of things from book publishing to rural planning and I hope to muck about with many more.

I used to want to write a book, but now I hope to start at the beginning and plant a forest.

Matriculated: 1978. *Graduated:* 1981. *Studied:* English Literature. *Lives in:* Bishampton, Worcestershire. *Works as:* Parish clerk. *Family:* Husband, Saul Jacka; two daughters, Anna (8 years) and Kate (5 years). *Car:* G-reg. VW Golf. *Income:* £1,416

Mark Johnson. I came to Trinity from Norwich City Technical College and from a family that had never sent anyone to university. I wasn't expecting much and Cambridge meant little to me although my initial distaste for the institution and the people was eventually mellowed by largely undemanding friendships and the pleasant – if bland – surroundings. The occasional resurfacing of 'media dons' in the Press reminds me, with a shiver, of just how trivial much of the institution was – with a few wonderful exceptions.

I had very little idea of direction or ambition at College and have gained

almost none since. I think I held on to adolescence in my work and relationships perhaps longer than most people do.

I am surprised perhaps by how things have turned out for me but, in truth, only mildly. It is all a little predictable – decent job, decent place to live, decent lifestyle – nothing too exciting. The next twenty years holds a, I hope gentle, decline.

Matriculated: 1979. *Graduated:* 1982.

Studied: History. *Lives in:* Islington, London. *Works as:* Editor of *Euroweek*, a financial magazine. *Family:* Girlfriend, no children. *Car:* None. *Income:* probably peaked this year

Nilufer Kheraj, Deborah Lawrenson, Louise Bell

Nilufer Kheraj. I am probably the last person to submit the narrative to accompany my photographs. Tardiness is symptomatic of my life when the demands of work impose themselves. At these times, I have no opportunity to concern myself with anything beyond the immediacy of the transaction I am working on and its implementation. Since my recent photograph was taken I have been shuttling from one transaction to the next and have been unconcerned about all else, including this piece. Did I realise this is how it would be as we sat with our picnic by the Cam? To me my ignorance is apparent

from the photograph! And yet, even then my ambition was to join Slaughter and May and make a career in the law. Despite the limitations it can impose on other aspects of my life, I enjoy my work immensely. Now I am (finally) to be married, I realise that there can be something more important to me than Slaughter and May. I hope my next twenty years will be filled with married life and children!

Matriculated: 1980. *Graduated:* 1983. *Studied:* Law. *Lives in:* Notting Hill, London. *Works as:* Solicitor. *Family:* None. *Car:* N-reg. BMW. *Income:* sufficient

Deborah Lawrenson. I look so calm in the old picture, yet I battled with debilitating nervousness that first year at Cambridge. It was sheer bravado that got me across Great Court on arrival and through the next months. I was on my own. My family had moved to Singapore and home was an empty house in South London.

Overawed by the university, I could have – should have – worked much harder. But I found college was one big party. This I could cope with. (Yes, please, to strange blue drinks and embarrassing clothes...) It all came together for me at the end. I fell in love, I worked for Finals and found I could still do it after all. I'd made friends in and out of college – Nilu and Louise in the picture are good friends to this day. It was an intense, exhilarating time. I trained as a journalist because I wanted to write (not that I admitted as much to anyone). I made it to Fleet Street at twenty-five. At Cambridge I'd never had the nerve to go to a Stop Press lunch. Then I stayed in a wonderfully ludicrous well-paid job on a gossip column, because I wanted to write. Eventually I

plundered it shamelessly for my first two novels.

At present I'm primarily a wife and mother. The man I met at Trinity was Robert Rees. We married in 1989, we have a two-year-old daughter, Madeleine, and we're happy. We live in idyllic countryside; materially we have far more than either of us ever expected.

My fourth novel is in progress and I want to write more than ever, but I have other priorities. I hope my publishers are right when they say that I'm a long-term bet for them.

Sometimes I feel unbearably lucky, as if all this might disappear as easily as it came. At other times I think no, I made it happen for myself, right from the

moment when, rigid with determination, I put my pen to the Cambridge Entrance papers.

Matriculated: 1980. *Graduated:* 1983. *Studied:* Modern Languages, then English. *Lives in:* Penshurst, Kent. *Works as:* Writer. *Family:* Husband, Robert; daughter, Madeleine (2 years). *Car:* Mercedes C200. *Income:* negligible this year

Jacquie Lindgren. I hadn't seen the 'then' picture before Mark came to do the 'now'. The setting, paraphernalia and knick-knacks certainly triggered memories. I feel essentially the same person now as then, in terms of principles, philosophy and beliefs. I'm a lot more confident and relaxed now however; perhaps less emotional in my unremitting wish that we all lived in a more just and humane world. Perhaps that will be reflected in the

second picture along with increase in wrinkles and decrease in clutter...

I was a little overwhelmed by Cambridge but had fun and am still in touch with the close friends I made then. When I left Trinity in 1981 I had no plan beyond 'wanting to work abroad'. A year's teacher training helped me achieve that; I have since spent many years in several educational guises in Asia and Africa. I have achieved two of my four

rather nebulous professional ambitions, namely to work for the United Nations and to take a higher degree at the School of Oriental and African Studies, University of London. I have also run my own mail order business, taught in prisons in London and been a management consultant. I am single although the designers of tick-box forms would prefer I labelled myself 'Divorced' or 'Living with Partner', both of which are

true. About three years ago someone I used to be at school with aged nine to eleven cycled past me. We recognised each other, a surprise which curbed my wanderlust, anchored me in North London and produced our son, now almost a year old. I never sought or yearned for motherhood and the emotion and joy that a baby has brought was quite unanticipated. I wonder how I will adapt now that I am less independent. Having

enjoyed the privileges of freedom and choice for so long, accepting compromise will be a significant challenge. Additionally, negotiating a rôle in a family setting is probably still more complex for middle-class women than it is for the majority of men.

I still don't think much beyond five years ahead. For me, I hope the next twenty years will be similar to the previous, filled with the indulgence of

books and travel and the pleasures provided by family, friends and sunshine. As for the more just and humane world…

Matriculated: 1978. *Graduated:* 1981. *Studied:* History. *Lives in:* Finsbury Park, London. *Works as:* Mother at the moment. *Family:* Rupert (partner) and one son, Herbert. *Car:* Never had one, never wanted one. *Income:* I have enough money to feel secure

Adrian Lucas. Reluctant to acknowledge myself in the old picture (like hearing my voice on a tape-recorder), I just guessingly sensed my contours. Was I alone in this reaction? Cambridge seemed Byronic to me, a Chateau for storytellers from Dickensian schools. But I had little to say, so Cambridge was Cha-Cha for me;

'Check-In! Chat-Chatte? Check-Out!' Had I known my fishier interests, I might have contributed a Shelleyan jelly-fish shock, or the Lacanic passion of a scorpion.

I grew up with skis, accomplices to drift through space and ride turns as they come; the Future some open space of possibility, the Past a weaving together of individual time-threads, and the Now some machinic conversion of space into time. Later I tried team sports with their space-control strategies, but I gave them up for books when we were taught how to win. Business is modelled on ball games and I can move along to their rituals, but my playing is just a Cha-Cha.

Never surprised by people in real life, I think surprise is a fictive device used by poor story-writers fixated on Identity. If we see Identity as the sum of our relationships with other people, then we are each more like massive tankers than sailing dinghies: 'love can't turn me 'round'.

One choice has been made: to say yes to a vegetarian way of life that I was born to, but which I rejected for many years. It's a decision to be intolerant in one aspect of life, and hopefully consummated by indulgence elsewhere.

Friends have lost close friends to death, and over the next years I will probably be exposed to this experience as well; I will blow the carry-on Cha-Cha one last cry, and start jobbing to the Danzòn.

Matriculated: 1978. *Graduated:* 1981. *Studied:* Natural Sciences. *Lives in:* Zug, Switzerland. *Works as:* Software business developer; partner in small company. *Family:* None. *Car:* ... ask me about my shoes ... *Income:* £50,000

Madeleine Marsh. After my lamentable A-Level results, it was luck that got me into Trinity. As requested I'd sent a photograph with my application form: blond curly hair all over the place, rainbow-coloured clothes (well it was the 1970s) and numerous hair ribbons. For Cambridge however my mother took decorative control. There I was waiting for my interview, hair in a viciously severe bun, brown tweed suit, flesh-coloured tights and ladylike gloves. 'Come in,' called the Director of Studies. He looked up, checked back with his papers (which unbeknownst to me included my picture) and stared at me through thick-rimmed spectacles. 'Are you sure you are feeling all right?' he asked pointedly. I subsequently discovered that the notes he took were nothing to do with my adolescent views on Tom Stoppard but were lines for a poem about how girls change when they want to get into Cambridge and my bum as I went out of the door.

I loved Cambridge. I'm afraid I did little work, partly because I read English and partly because in my first term I fell in love with a fellow Trinity student, Jon Lewin, who is now my husband. When I wasn't lying in bed watching Tiswas and eating toast burnt on the gas fire, I acted and sang in bands and had a good time with my friends.

I have however worked very hard ever since. Since I was a child I have loved antiques. After Cambridge, I took a course in the decorative arts and then set up my own company researching the history of problem works of art. I am now the editor of *Millers Collectables Price Guide* (the collector's bible). I am also a presenter for *The Antiques Show* on BBC2. In theory at least this is a part-time career, because I have an eight-year-old son Joshua, no nanny and I divide my time between running round the park pretending to be a dinosaur and trying to be professional. Like every other part-time working mum, I veer between thinking I have the best of both worlds and worrying that I am rubbish at both of them. I am very lucky. I have a great family and a fascinating job. I have no idea what the next twenty years might hold. Next year however my publishers want me to write a book on collecting the 1970s, so one thing I do know is that we're all becoming antiques.

Matriculated: 1979. Graduated: 1982. Studied: English Literature. Lives in: Hammersmith, London. *Works as:* Aniques writer, broadcaster. *Family:* Husband, Jon Lewin; son Joshua (8 years). *Car:* Can't drive, see you on the Piccadilly line. *Income:* What a rude question! Not as much as if I had a proper job

Richard Meredith. I am not sure I remember much about the circumstances of these Cambridge photographs. Why I was running towards Mark is now lost to me. I look a bit of a prat. But my memory for this sort of thing has always been tactfully short. The picture of the party (page 78) was taken in the function rooms above the ICA at a party given by a Francesca Denman. I remember the name as I do a nursery school chum but nothing else. I am evidently far too young to be drinking. For the recent photo, Mark came to stay with us when we were in Bonn. I think I look a bit of a prat there too, but the unifying feature across the years is that I have never liked having my photograph taken.

Cambridge was for me the usual adolescent cocktail of laziness and emotional turbulence. As a place or an institution, it exacts little sentimental pull now. But it set some things on rocks.

It gave me a circle of friends that has remained and grown into an extended family. Beyond everything, it was the time when I met my wife.

After Cambridge, life has been more a question of lucky drift rather than tactical planning. After a year of postgraduate study in America, I joined the Diplomatic Service and have done this now for sixteen years. We have lived for seven years in the Caribbean, Central America, and

Germany and I have travelled widely in Southern Africa, the US and Europe. Living abroad imposes its irritations. But it has tended in the main to keep life colourful and London (and friends) fresh. My job has put me into the role of peripheral spear-carrier in some great political dramas. It is instructive to see politicians up close. As my decision to take permanent employment of any sort was at the time largely dictated by short-term whim and financial pressure, I have been very lucky to end up doing something I am still enthused by. Perhaps I have an increasingly contented nature.

But like most people, I work too hard for too little. And hate the quickening disappearance of time.

My other interests nurtured by Cambridge (music, theatre, aimless chatting) die a bit more each year.

We now have two children.

When we have been back in the UK we have shifted around houses in Fulham before departing this year to live in Buckinghamshire. We also have a small holiday house in France, bought with a Cambridge friend.

Matriculated: 1979. *Graduated:* 1982. *Studied:* History. *Lives in:* Gerrards Cross, Buckinghamshire. *Works as:* Diplomat. *Family:* Married, two daughters. *Car:* VW Passat 93. *Income:* not disclosed

Louisa Oriel, Alexandra Poulovassilis, Richard Meredith

Louisa Oriel. I remember wanting to be at Trinity because of its architecture. When I think back on Cambridge now that is still what I think of. People move on but I know that the sunsets over the Wren Library are still spectacular. Initially I felt the College was too male and Public School. Later I didn't care and got on with my own thing. Friends, films, drinking and talking. Happily most of these including the friends have stayed with me. One of them became my husband.

Since Cambridge I have worked for Shell which so far has had the decency to tolerate periods of absence whilst we live abroad in the course of Richard's job in the Diplomatic Service. Living and travelling in the Caribbean, Nicaragua, Central and South America, and Germany have only partially made up for the intermittent career breaks. The sunnier the climate and the better the beaches the less I seem to mind about it. At least I have had the chance to do the full-time mother rôle

with our two young daughters for three years before working full-time again.

It is still tough to have two reasonable careers and children. Whilst abroad I have somewhat half-heartedly done the Diplomatic wife bit. This is often dull or silly. It is rarely sexist as it used occasionally to be. What it does do is give a period-ic injection of new and sometimes foreign friends that in London one seems to have no energy to make. I also now speak bad Spanish and even worse German and our children can order their apple juice in three different languages. Well almost. As we have just returned from Bonn to live in Gerrards Cross they won't get much practice for a few years anyway.

Matriculated: 1979. *Graduated:* 1982. *Studied:* History. *Lives in:* Gerrards Cross, Buckinghamshire. *Works as:* Human resources manager. *Family:* Married, two daughters. *Car:* VW Passat 93. *Income:* some would think it too much, most would think it too little

Alexandra Poulovassilis. I was very pleased to see the picture Mark took. Cambridge has mixed memories for me. I had some very good friends there, but my family had recently returned to Greece and I felt I was in a kind of cultural no-man's-land, feeling neither British nor Greek (I'd spent very little of my life in Greece up to then, but had had a fairly typical Greek family life in Britain) Happily, all of this resolved itself after Cambridge, when I returned to Greece and worked at IBM for three years. My job involved a certain amount of travel, and meeting a variety of people and cultures helped me to better understand myself as a mixture of various influences. As I now have a daughter who has triple nationality (British, Greek and Iranian) it is just as well that I'm managing to cope with my two! I returned to Britain in 1985, to do a MSc and then a PhD in Computer Science. I met my husband while we were research students at Birkbeck College, and

we were married in 1992. My brother had a serious accident in 1993 and was in and out of hospital for two and a half years, most of that time in London. We spent as much time with him as possible and postponed starting a family until he had recovered. Our daughter Maria was born in August 1996 and changed our lives, naturally. After finishing my PhD in 1989, I was a Postdoctoral Fellow at University College, London until 1991, and then joined King's College, London as a Lecturer. I was promoted to Senior Lecturer in 1997. I enjoy the work and I am not at all surprised that this is how things have turned out. I find the variety and intellectual challenge of the job appealing. I will not be surprised if I remain an academic.

Matriculated: 1979. *Graduated:* 1982. *Studied:* Mathematics. *Lives in:* Hertford, Herts. *Works as:* Academic. *Family:* Husband, Mir, 36, Software architect; daughter Maria (2 years). *Car:* Toyota Carina 2.0. *Income:* £33,500

Bernd Meyer Witting. The photo was taken in the Trinity Fellows' Garden during May Week in my last year at Trinity. It conjured up visions of the final social events of life at Cambridge – May Balls, May Bumps and Graduation. After that, farewell to a whole way of life and to many friends, only a few of whom I have kept in touch over the last twenty years.

Cambridge was significant in that it marked a real step into freedom after the strictly regimented public school I had attended. At Trinity, there was time for extra-curricular activities, whether social or sporting. In Cambridge, it didn't seem to matter where you came from, more important was who you were and what you did, which I found tremendously refreshing.

Then: a three month trip to South-East Asia and the start of my German law studies at the University of Erlangen. The contrast with Cambridge could not have been starker. Erlangen had terrible facilities both academically and recreationally. At Cambridge we had regular supervisions with one academic to three to four students. Now we just had lectures and occasional working groups of over thirty students taught by a very junior academic. There was no campus to provide a social focus.

The choice to return to Germany after

Trinity was my most significant. My Cambridge peers qualified six or seven years before me. I watched while they found fame and fortune in the real world back in England but I never regretted that decision.

I had always hoped to be a lawyer in an international environment, so it did not come as a particular surprise that I should end up with Clifford Chance, one of the very few truly international law firms. Perhaps the real surprise is that I might not have ended up there, had it not been for the encouragement of some old friends from Trinity.

Who knows what the next twenty years will hold. Professionally, I think that we will see an increasing globalisation of the legal market and more and more reliance on information technology in our daily work.

Matriculated: 1978. *Graduated:* 1981. *Studied:* Law. *Lives in:* Kelkheim, near Frankfurt. *Works as:* Partner, Clifford Chance Frankfurt. *Family:* Wife, (Christl Meyer-Witting, *née* Wildenauer, married 1990) and one daughter Sophie (4 years). *Car:* BMW (what else, with my initials?). *Income:* not disclosed

Richard Neville. There was a village on the edge of a forest in which a nightingale sang. Every evening the villagers would hear its voice but no one had ever seen it. One day a young man went into the forest. He heard the voice of the bird and followed it as it receded into the depths. He followed it all day and still could not see it. In the middle of the forest he met an old man sitting under an oak tree. 'Have you seen a nightingale?', he asked. 'Of course,' said the old man, 'but first you must go to the woodcutter's cottage and bring me a glass of water.'

The young man went to the cottage and the woodcutter's daughter answered the door. He immediately fell in love with her. He courted her and eventually they married. The young man lived in the cottage. He and his wife had several children.

Years passed and one day they decided to move to the city. It was an arduous journey. Before they reached the city they were attacked by robbers and everybody was killed except for the young man. He was sold into slavery far away from home.

He began to rebuild his life and impressed his master so much that he rose to become his trusted advisor.

He even married his master's daughter and once again he prospered. Years passed and the river that ran through the city began to flood. A great tidal wave spread out and destroyed everything in its path. The man watched as it tore his wife and children from his grasp.

He himself was carried on the wave for mile after mile until he caught hold of a tree and saved himself. He found himself in a forest and began to crawl along, half dead.

Eventually he collapsed in the shade of an oak tree. Then he heard a voice. 'I sent you to get me a glass of water two hours ago, why have you been so long?' The man opened his eyes. There was the old man smiling. Then he turned into a nightingale and flew away.

Matriculated: 1978. *Graduated:* 1981. *Studied:* Mathematics. *Lives in:* Dartmouth Park, North London. *Works as:* Storyteller. *Family:* Single, no children. *Car:* None. *Income:* not disclosed

Tom Oates. After graduation I decided to pursue my career as an Eco-warrior. However my campsite at Twyford Down was fifteen years ahead of its time, and I was unable to generate the level of publicity necessary for producing a lucrative autobiography. I was therefore compelled, much to my regret, to seek employment in the tawdry world of commerce. Wonderbra had been pursuing me for some time to help them develop their interests in the Far East, so I spent the next two years setting up a regional headquarters in Bali. Unfortunately, sales in the region failed to match expectations,

and my employers and I agreed to part. The City of London has now become my commercial field of operations, although I remain in touch with my emotions through my highly rewarding writing contract for Mills and Boon, under the critically acclaimed pseudonym of Lisa Best. When not occupied with the above, I divide my time between my three wives and twenty-three children at my beach hut in Bali and my villa in Wigan.

Matriculated: 1978. *Graduated:* 1981. *Studied:* Law Part Ia, Classics Part II. *Lives in:* Leicestershire. *Works as:* Fund manager. *Family:* Yes. *Car:* Yes. *Income:* not disclosed

Julian Parker. I'd forgotten I still had some hair left then: I thought it had mostly gone before I left Trinity. I'd have liked to stay in archaeology, but only one of my friends ever achieved that. I guessed an accounting firm might take in an unemployed archaeologist, so I drifted into qualifying as an accountant at Grant Thornton. I gravitated towards forensic accountancy since many of the analytical skills needed are very similar to archaeological ones.

My mother became very ill in 1993 and in 1994 my father died. Mother couldn't cope on her own, so I moved back to help my sister look after her: fortunately the house is big enough to have enabled me to convert the top floor into a flat where Ann and I now live. Marcus Beale, who I met in my first week at Trinity, was the architect: it amuses me that an apparently

chance meeting twenty years ago led to the two of us designing the flat in a wine bar. If I hadn't received a chance phone call from a colleague in 1990 I probably wouldn't be at the SFO and I might not be married: the call led to a successful investigation and prosecution, which led to my move to the SFO, where I met Ann. No one at the office had spotted that we'd even noticed one another until the Daily Telegraph City Diary leaked our wedding the day we got married. I'm not sure either of us thought we'd ever get married, but now we can't imagine what it would be like not to be.

Matriculated: 1978. *Graduated:* 1982. *Studied:* Part I Classics, Part II Archaeology. *Lives in:* Crouch End, London. *Works as:* Principal financial investigator, Serious Fraud Office. *Family:* Wife, Ann. *Car:* Volvo. *Income:* enough

Michael Perry. As a child, I lived only an hour away from Cambridge. My Oxford-educated aunt often took me there for the day. It was fairly obvious indoctrination into the rewards for hard work at school but I also learnt another lesson; Cambridge was more about quiet pleasures like picnics and punting. I do not think this was a bad thing. I now go through life with phases of intense work followed by reverie. Your earlier photograph caught me in one of my quiet phases.

Aside from being a huge treat, Cambridge was also confident enough of its selection policy that I was allowed to change from Engineering to History during my second term. This saved me from spending my whole life following a

professional career and encouraged me to try doing as many things as I could. It also gave me the confidence to believe that everything is possible. Having just left the investment bank where I spent my last twelve years, I am about to find out whether this is true when you work alone. Whatever, provided I can continue this pattern of work and play, I believe I shall at least be content.

Matriculated: 1979. *Graduated:* 1983. *Studied:* History. *Lives in:* Greenwich, London. *Works as:* Inventor and journey-man banker. *Family:* Married Emily Patrick (New Hall 1978-1982) in 1986. We have three children, Beatrice (11 years), Isabel (8 years) and Alfred (4 years). *Car:* One. *Income:* no salary

Sue Porter. Memories of Trinity: Buck's Fizz in the Fellows' Gardens; black tie 'do's' in the Old Kitchens; beers in Trinity bar; sweaty nights bopping in the Wolfson party room; losing the small hours putting the world to rights in someone's room, somewhere ... hangovers in the Trinity law library. How did Mark manage to find a photo of me looking reasonably studious, and how did I get that law degree, I wonder?

Obviously, life changed a bit after Cambridge – less Buck's Fizz in the Gardens and more beers down the pub – but many of the friends made then remain good friends today and I have persevered with the law. I decided to qualify as a solicitor principally for lack of any other inspiration but, somewhat to my surprise, found that I really enjoyed tax law. I have specialised in this area since qualification, remaining at Freshfields, where I have been a partner for the last five years or so, throughout. I think the appeal of this particular career lay in the combined lure of a technically challenging subject and a working environment where enthusiasm for a spot of partying is a definite asset.

On the personal side, I managed to

remain free and single long after the young bit could apply, but, just when I (and, no doubt, long-suffering friends) had become resigned to my future as a particularly self-indulgent and cantankerous spinster, I met Peter, who I married two years ago. Since then we have bought a house in Putney, West London, which we have had a lot of fun doing up, acquired Pushkin the cat (pictured next to me on the sofa) and produced a daughter, Emily (pictured as a bump in the sofa shot).

These recent events have wrought some serious changes in my lifestyle: beers down the pub have now made way for coffee mornings with the NCT mums in Putney. I remain Sue Porter at work (and I do intend to go back after my maternity leave) but I'm now quite used to being Mrs de Salis as well, and am gradually coming to terms with the awesome responsibility of motherhood. Who knows what the next twenty years will bring, but I am certain that they will be quite different to the last.

Matriculated: 1978. *Graduated:* 1981. *Studied:* Law. *Lives in:* Putney, West London. *Works as:* Tax lawyer. *Family:* Married; one daughter. *Car:* Rarely used. *Income:* more than Annabel Sykes

Sarah Robertson. Looking at the old photos from Trinity, I just thought how much fun Cambridge was. I have no recollection of hard work, stress or pressure, just many evenings spent in the bar, talking or playing cards until dawn. This may have contributed to not very good results in Veterinary Medicine in my first year. I changed to Economics, because becoming a vet seemed to involve far too many years of hard work, and chose Economics because Law was full!

At that I age I think we all felt invincible and that we would undoubtedly be the best at whatever we chose. Perhaps that is the biggest gift that Cambridge gives you – I've certainly never used my Economics degree. Having had no specific plans or goals on leaving Trinity, where I am now is not a surprise. The major change in my life was at twenty-seven. Having spent six years in advertising and become a director of London's largest media buyer, I decided to take a year out. I'd enjoyed my time abroad between school and university so much that I decided the time to do it again was then, not when I would be too old to enjoy it. I took a job in Switzerland training show-jumpers for a millionaire – who happened to be the Amateur show-jumping champion of Switzerland. Winters in St Moritz, private helicopter, and his own airline – that's

seriously rich! It was a fantastic two years.

Since the early 1990s I have been in business for myself. Saatchi & Saatchi had bought my old employer by the time I returned to the UK and I didn't fancy becoming another rat on a very large wheel. After a few false starts and backward steps, I now have a company that is successful and, in the age of information technology, transportable. This has allowed me to move to France with my partner where we have purchased three properties to renovate and let, leaving plenty of time for 'just eating some cheese, drinking some wine and soaking up some rays' – and lots of golf. Like most of the rest of my choices since leaving Trinity this was spur of the moment, not part of a master plan.

The future – who knows – but, please God, anything but a 'proper job'.

Matriculated: 1978. Graduated: 1981.

Studied: Veterinary Medicine in first year and Economics in second and third years. *Lives in:* Longué-Jumelles, Maine et Loire, France. *Works as:* Own company supplying products to 'QVC – The Shopping Channel' in the UK & Germany. *Family:* Living with Nigel since 1991. No children, but he has two daughters. *Car:* Black Saab Turbo 9000 and white Volkswagen panel van. *Income:* if it were enough, I'd have retired long ago

Andrew Roxburgh. Mark showed me two photographs. Obviously I chose the one here, the close-up of myself looking very confident and self-important as befits a student. I now realise how lucky I was to go to Trinity, although the medical course was a bit too academic (I did not enjoy anatomy exams!) and mostly irrelevant to clinical reality. I qualified in 1984 at St. Bartholomew's Hospital in London. I now work in Kent as a General Practitioner in a partnership of six. I have had to choose between continuing to climb up the greasy pole of hospital medicine (kow-towing to consultants!) and general practice – I do not now regret my choice.

I enjoy tennis and swimming at a nearby country club in summer and

shooting in Kent in the winter.

My current projects are: to manage a major upgrade to our information technology at work and keep all the partners happy; continuing renovations to our house (the plumbers are installing a new central heating system at present) and planning my fortieth birthday celebrations.

Matriculated: 1978. *Graduated:* 1981. *Studied:* Medicine. *Lives in:* Sevenoaks, Kent. *Works as:* General Practitioner.

Family: Wife, Roz who studied Physiology at Bristol and works as a tax accountant at PriceWaterhouseCoopers; Rachael (4 years), Venetia (3 years) and Eleanor (nearly 2); 'Teal' black Labrador. *Car:* Yes. *Income:* not disclosed

Charles Roxburgh and Karen Pierce
(*overleaf*). What did I think looking at the
'old' picture? How fast nearly twenty
years have gone by and how awful my
glasses were.

What did Cambridge mean to me? Cold
winter mornings on the river, breakfast in
Hall, coffee in the University Library,
lunch at Wolfson Court, Fitzbillies cakes,
Spanish Castle, discos in the Wolfson
building, wet summer evenings on the
river, Pimms in the Fellows' Garden,
stilettos on wet grass, drinks parties in
Old Kitchen, bicycles chained outside
Great Gate, the Great Court run, sweet
sherry at tutorials, earnest discussions
late at night – and three years went by
so fast. Do where I am or what I am
doing surprise me? I had no idea what I
would do after Cambridge. I am not
surprised, as the outcome is all rather
conventional.

Did I make any significant choices
along the way? What is surprising is how

just a few decisions have shaped the way our lives have turned out. The early career choices on leaving Cambridge have had a huge impact on our lives, but at the time we didn't treat these as 'life shaping' decisions at all. So the big decisions have been... getting married; for Karen, my wife, going into the Foreign Office rather than accepting an offer from an accountancy firm; for me, deciding to go to Business School, after three dull years at Andersen consulting, and then joining McKinsey; moving to Washington in 1992. I have no idea what the next twenty years hold.

Matriculated: 1978. Graduated: 1981.

Studied: Charles – Classics; Karen (Girton) – English. *Lives in:* Chelsea, London. *Works as:* Charles – Management Consultant; Karen – Foreign Office. *Family:* Two sons, Tom (7 years) and Jack (1 year). *Car:* Volvo Estate; Fiat Punto. *Income:* Karen – not very much; Charles – more

Karen Pierce

Charles Roxburgh, Karen Pierce

Gavin Ryan. Looking back on my time at Cambridge I now have a fond memory because, luckily for me, it was only one of a number of life experiences rather than a defining moment. I don't look back and pine for those days; but do remember some of the friendships I developed. Some of these went on and others did not – that's life.

Like many others, ever since leaving I have been more or less permanently in that great British industry, financial services, apart from a brief stint in the Foreign Office and some dabbling in the movie industry a few years ago. I have been doing mostly international work and for the last few years have specialised in the Balkan countries. Unlike many in my industry who moan forever but never do anything else, I am fortunate to enjoy what I do immensely mainly, I think, because I made some risky choices which have (I think) finally paid off. Cambridge certainly did not teach me to do that!

I spend most of my time in and around Belgrade and keep a base in London. I was married for three years to an Italian lady and have a four-year-old son, Nicholas, who I try to see as much as I can, which can be difficult as he lives in Milan with his mother.

Looking at my picture of the time, I thought I looked better! At my ten-year reunion I was surprised by how trim and fit most people looked – better than when we were then. Must be all the salads and mineral water we have to consume now we are all over thirty-five.

Would I encourage my son or daughter to go? On balance, yes but I would make them sell used cars in their holidays!

Matriculated: 1980. *Graduated:* 1984. *Studied:* Part I Engineering, Part II Modern & Medieval Languages. *Lives in:* London and Belgrade. *Works as:* Investment banker. *Family:* Separated, one boy (4 years). *Car:* none. *Income:* mostly in shaky currencies

John Scott. I don't feel older after twenty years, but I do feel very different – a lot more comfortable with me as a person, a lot less worried about being what other people want me to be. I always felt very self-aware, even at eighteen, but I used it destructively then – in self-criticism – whereas now I've accepted that I'll not change some things about myself and I use that self-awareness positively.

I never really planned to go to Cambridge, arriving almost by accident. It was a shock to discover there were people much brighter than me, but it also gave me the first big challenge I'd ever faced – to prove I could succeed at that level. Meeting that challenge gave me a lot confidence I'd never needed before, but I think the most important thing it taught me was quality of effort beats quantity (well –most of the time at least). I've clung to that lesson ever since, and it has really helped me to balance work, family and personal interests over the years. I might even be the first person to have 'I wish I'd spent more time at the office' as my epitaph.

Given that, I am surprised to have reached such a senior position in my profession. I envy people who seem to know where they're going – life for me is a surprise to experience. There have been a couple of major turning points where

I've definitely made the right choice – leaving my first company, working overseas, getting engaged on the second date – and a couple where I got it wrong. Best not to dwell on those. Overall I feel incredibly fortunate to have material comfort, a loving family, and a small measure of financial security – and enough disposable income to go sports-car racing a few times a year.

Regrets – a few, mostly I wish I had more time (in several meanings of the phrase) for friends and relationships. I might see my children growing up, but I can see myself as a lonely old man one day. In twenty-two years I'll be sixty – the age my father died. I keep reminding my-self to live for today, not to look forward to a retirement I might never have. I'll let my children be my achievement and my life, hopefully, its own reward.

Matriculated: 1978. Graduated: 1982.

Studied: Chemical Engineering. *Lives in:* the Worcester countryside surrounded by corn and fruit trees. *Works as:* Director of Albright & Wilson (UK) Ltd, a subsidiary of chemical company Albright & Wilson Plc. *Family:* Married to Sarah for thirteen years and plead guilty to Daniel (8 years) and James (6 years). *Cars:* Drive a hot Golf and race a Porsche. *Income:* more than a cabinet minister but always manage to spend it all

Tim Smith. My thoughts on seeing the Trinity photograph were: 'I'm sure I didn't graduate in the 70s!' and – 'were the Cambridge days really as carefree as the image suggests?' As for the first thought – I realised very soon that I very nearly did! As for the second thought – surrounded now by bankers' boxes, with files that needed doing weeks ago and the prospect of an all-night session of work ahead I suppose there can only be one answer!

Having left Trinity determined on a career at the Bar I have only had to make two real 'career choices' – the first was whether to carry on at all after completing pupillage and the second was whether to move to Manchester or stay in London. I carried on – and I moved. To date both have proved to be the right choices.

Although perhaps inevitably one sometimes thinks 'what if I had done x, y, z...' – fortunately the posing of this question is occasioned only out of mild curiosity and not out of any sense of regret at the decisions taken.

As for other so-called 'life choices' one of the most important was my decision to sell my MG Midget. With part of the proceeds I went on a holiday to Portugal

and there had the good fortune to meet my wife! Having met, one of the most important decisions to be taken came very easily – to get married. In fact this seemed to be the most natural thing in the world – so much so that looking back I don't recall a great deal of actual choice in fact being exercised.

My three more recent and most important 'choices' have resulted in Rowland,
Angharad and Huw. Again choice played very little part in what were very natural decisions. However choice (and care!) plays a greater role in restricting the offspring to three.

Whatever expectations I may have had of life when at Trinity – I am sure that they have been fulfilled – even if not in the precise ways that I might have imagined. I hope that I can be so
lucky in the next twenty years.

Matriculated: 1978. Graduated: 1981. Studied: Law. Lives in: Alderley Edge, Cheshire. Works as: Barrister. Family: Wife, Sian; 3 children – Rowland (6 years), Angharad (4 years) and Huw (2 years). *Car:* Saab 1993 cabriolet. *Income:* not disclosed

Annabel Sykes. Then...my strongest and best memories...nothing to do with the law, which I found a deep disappointment as an academic subject. Nor to do with the men who thought I wasn't equal just because I was female (my first experience of this coming from an all-girls' school and a majority female family).

Meeting people who were totally different from anyone I had ever met before. Here Juliet Peston really stands out. She fed me roast pepper salad about ten years before it became the restaurant staple it is today. She taught me to go to restaurants as a pastime and not just an extravagant treat and sorted out my woolly politics. She became, and remains, a dear friend.

Falling in love for the first time ... and being unhappily wrenched out of it. More extremes of emotion than I'd ever felt before.

The chance to do so many different things. Rowing, theatre, cinema, eating out, drinking out, so many parties, so many boat club and other dinners, so many friends. Terrible hangovers after too much port. Terrible tears after too much whisky. The breath-taking beauty of Great Court on a misty autumn

evening. The incredible, careless privilege of it all.

And now? I feel that I have been incredibly lucky. I met Richard at Law School and have lived with him since late 1984. I started at Freshfields in 1985 and am still there with a lot of good friends among my partners and colleagues. I have always enjoyed law in a practical context and have been fortunate in finding a niche as a regulatory lawyer. This brings me interesting and varied work and meant I was fortunate (or unfortunate) enough, depending on which way you look at it (given that it was definitely the most stressful time of my life) to be heavily involved in the reconstruction and renewal of the Lloyd's insurance market.

Will I still be doing this when I am fifty? No. When I am forty? Probably, but not too long after that.

Matriculated: 1979. *Graduated:* 1982. *Studied:* Law. *Lives in:* Regents Park, London. *Works as:* Partner of Freshfields. *Family:* Unmarried, no children yet. *Car:* Several. *Income:* Less than Sue Porter but enough to make very early retirement a serious possibility

Richard Thomas. This picture was taken not in Cambridge but in Oxford on a visit we made for a dinner in my third year. At the time I had no idea what I wanted to do after graduation and in fact left Cambridge without having a job lined up. After six months doing nothing I drifted into a job in the City which, given the growth since then in financial markets, was an extremely lucky choice. Three years ago I moved to Tokyo and expect to be based here until I retire. As

they say in this business – annually – 'just one more year'.

    Matriculated: 1978. *Graduated:* 1981. *Studied:* Mathematics Part Ia, Philosophy Part II. *Lives in:* Tokyo. *Works as:* Investment banker. *Family:* Wife, Motoko; daughter, Thea (1 year). *Car:* Porsche and Mercedes. *Income:* not disclosed

Pip Torrens. The old picture shows a full head of hair above an unlined face of bovine arrogance. I was aware that Cambridge would be a qualified squandering of opportunity and that that was how it should be. I never really thought about the future in remotely 'realistic' terms, which is something of a prerequisite for an actor. So there has been no change there. My most significant choice would be going to Roddy Williams' house in Bethnal Green in 1992 where I met my wife and subsequently experienced more life in four years than I had in the previous eleven.

The next twenty years, if the inverted career pattern of the typical actor prevails, will, I hope see a progressive lapse out of retirement into continuous projects of indignity and profit.

Matriculated: 1978. *Graduated:* 1981. *Studied:* English Literature. *Lives in:* Peckham Rye, London. *Works as:* Actor. *Family:* Wife, Chantal Krishnadasan, Barrister; daughters Lanikai (4 years) and Elysia (1 year). *Car:* 1993 Volkswagen Golf. *Income:* variable, enormously

Steve Wallace. The photograph demonstrates the leading edge sense of style and fashion for which Trinity mathematicians are well-known.

My memory of Cambridge is of having greater freedom to choose how to spend my time than I have known before or since. I regret the extra financial burden placed on today's generation of students, as higher education is one of those things for which I would happily pay more in taxes.

Most of my working time since graduation has been spent in Information Technology, which is no surprise, given that I had experience of it before coming up in 1978. Despite causing my parents some grief by switching from maths to philosophy after the first year, I would say that philosophy has provided the best possible grounding for business and

domestic life. The DIY in our house, for example, is a testament to the Popperian ideal of learning by making mistakes as fast as possible.

My aim to take time off to do research has not yet been achieved, but I plan to be able to do this before I'm fifty.

Meanwhile, my most important project is the welfare of my family, and especially my children, who are likely to increase in their numbers and demands in the near future.

Matriculated: 1978. *Graduated:* 1981. *Studied:* Part 1a Mathematics, Part II

Philosophy. *Lives in:* Wargrave, Berkshire. *Works as:* IT consultant, NCR Ltd. *Family:* Wife, Paula; Alfie (3 years), Martha (1 year). *Car:* 1991 Sierra Estate. *Income:* less than I'd like, more than I deserve

Alan Weir. Biography, in contrast to this, was easy – raise your hand all those not tempted to show searing insight into the past or savvy analysis of the present. If you expect to be blinded by the light, give up now.

The spartan details. Law School was the Badlands – Surrey was as dreary as Nebraska, but survivable. Growing up in a firm of City solicitors, ditto. (Not dreary, but survival threatened by a youthful lack of tact). Independence Day came with their offer of partnership in 1991. While it's hard to be a saint in the City, if the client will cover me for the fee and isn't a fully paid-up resident of the darkness on the edge of town, I'd admit to enjoying the occasional war. The seeds of those are usually sown in the backstreets of the insurance world. Is it where I thought, in the glory days, I would now be? If not, it's a pretty near miss.

A different story domestically. The smart money said I'd marry a Jersey girl, and certainly not anyone English, let alone that she, whatever her nationality, could put up with me for this long. Fi must just be tougher than the rest. She has given us a daughter with only a slight trace of her father's personality – Adam raised a

Cainette, I suppose – and a son whose motto (at the age of two) seems to be No Surrender. Must be the luck of the Irish.

Irish? And thereby hangs the tale, or rather that biography. My hometown attic disgorged bundles of letters written by a Great War soldier, my grandfather, once believed to be as Canadian as Mounties and maple syrup. It now seems that he regarded himself as Irish. The five years it took to write a short account of his life on the Western Front is living proof that I never could have cut the mustard as an historian, however hard Walter Ullmann tried. The next twenty should tell whether Tony, Gareth Jones et al. get a better return for their efforts.

And Cambridge? That's simple – none of us had the slightest idea how lucky we were. Well, I did say there would be no searing insights and no, my musical tastes would not seem to have changed much. For those who have guessed the question, the answer there is nineteen.

Matriculated: 1978. *Graduated:* 1982. *Studied:* History and Law. *Lives in:* Blackheath, London. *Works as:* Partner of Ince & Co, Solicitors. *Family:* Fi, Joanna and Ralph. *Cars:* MX5 1.8i. A6 TDI SE. *Income:* not disclosed

David Womersley. I arrived for the first time in Cambridge when I attended for interview in a snow-bound December. Waking up on the morning of my interview, I discovered that I had forgotten to pack a razor. Lathered up in the chair of the barber in St. John's Passage, cut-throat blade poised over my throat, I was asked by far the most nonplussing question of the day: 'Tell me, Sir – do you believe in God?'. Whatever answer I gave, it was clearly the right one, and after that the interview seemed a less daunting prospect. But it did take me a while to calm down. In fact, I didn't manage it until my third year as an undergraduate, when I shared a set in New Court with Roy Williams.

Looking back, it's clear that I owe so

much to Trinity. The chance to meet my wife, of course, and all the intellectual benefits that came from being taught by Adrian Poole, Leo Salingar and Theo Redpath. Less obviously, I now see that my years at Trinity were pivotal, and that the immense self-sufficiency of the College, by which I was at first abashed, in the end I found invigorating. Trinity equipped me to enter, eventually, into possession of myself.

Matriculated: 1976. *Graduated:* 1979. *Studied:* English. *Left Trinity:* 1981.

Lives in: Oxford. *Works as:* Fellow and Tutor in English, Jesus College, Oxford. *Family:* Wife, Caro (Trinity 1979); Children, James (12 years), Kate (10 years), Rachel (6 years). *Car:* S-reg. Discovery. *Income:* £65,000

Sarah Woodward. The first thing that struck me when I saw the photo of me at Trinity was 'my God, I know that look – it's my mother's!' I'm even wearing her locket. I look sweet and innocent, when I certainly wasn't. I also look a lot thinner, which I certainly was.

I had an extraordinary time at Cambridge but the academic side of it seemed a little superfluous. When I got my degree my tutor told me I had destroyed his belief in the education system and I'm certainly more interested in history and anthropology today than I was then. No, Cambridge was for parties, sex, drink and drugs, with the occasional fight thrown in, and I had absolutely no idea what to do when it was over. I even considered a PhD, to my tutor's utter horror.

I ended up selling wine in Paris but when I ran out of money I was lured into management consultancy and it took me six years to get out again. Just as I was about to sign the partnership papers I thought, 'this isn't what life is all about' and did a runner. My time at Trinity gave me the confidence to think I could earn money some more enjoyable way. Of course, if I'd stayed at The Coba Group I'd be rather rich by now.

Two years after I left Trinity I married a man I had met while I was there, to many

people's amazement – I think including his. But although I have been married for thirteen years, many of my contemporaries seem more married than I am, probably because they have children. Children haven't happened for us but if they had we wouldn't have gone down the Grand Trunk Road on an Enfield Bullet or trekked amongst the Stone Age people of Irian Jaya.

Who knows which is better, but today life seems to have come full circle. I travel three or four months a year, I get books out from the University Library and have 'essay crises' over articles, I quite often stay up until four in the morning drinking and smoking too much, and am often broke. What is weird is that quite often more responsible friends say 'you're so lucky.' Well, it's not luck, it's choice.

Matriculated: 1980. Graduated: 1983.

Studied: Archaeology and Anthropology Part I; History Part II. *Lives in:* A state of excessive untidiness in a house in Bow, London, currently shared with a dog and a cat. *Works as:* Food writer, travel photographer, editor and when I am really broke as a management consultant. *Family:* Married Jonathan Gregson in 1985. *Car:* Irrelevant question. *Income:* best described as fluctuating

Jocelyn Wyburd. When I saw the photo I thought: 'well that's just typical, I'd only been there a week, my room's a mess and there are two men in it!'. Some things don't change, I still live and work in a mess, although I'm perceived to be very organised and productive. But there are no men in my life at the moment, though a few have passed through along the way.

Trinity for me was about drinking and rowing (I was temporarily known as the boat-club alcoholic) and enjoying being around men after single-sex schooling. I got a good degree on the side, mainly because I enjoyed my subject, certainly not because I did very much work. I never thought about the learning process at all at that time. Since re-training as a teacher, studying a Masters degree part-time and working in the development of learning methods and materials through technology, it seems I've come a long way.

I never knew what I would do, but somehow assumed I would slip into some intellectually fulfilling career, get married, have children and live a comfortable home counties life like my mother. I didn't expect any of that to be difficult to achieve as I'd always achieved whatever with the minimum of effort.

Since Trinity I've had more careers than most, from education and development

in Nepal to fund-raising and event organising with Sport Aid, international management consultancy, temping, teaching and now educational development. I've lived in Sicily, Nepal, London, Gateshead and Hull. I have no particular roots and seem still to be looking for that new challenge on the horizon. It is the journey I enjoy; when I get there I always want to move on.

I'm still waiting for the biological clock to start ticking, but am increasingly convinced that it won't. Not desirous of becoming a mother (and having a surrogate child in the form of my dog) I have not felt pressured into settling down in a relationship. It can be lonely at times, but I'm not prepared to compromise my independence just to have any old person around!

Matriculated: 1980. *Graduated:* 1984. *Studied:* Italian and French (with year abroad in Sicily). *Lives in:* Hull. *Works as:* Senior learning adviser (Modern Languages). *Employer:* University of Lincolnshire & Humberside. *Family:* Zak (border collie/ greyhound/terrier rescue dog – female). *Unions:* in various jobs, and to varying degrees of activism: NUT, NATFHE, Unison. *Interests:* travel, walking, the gym. *Vices:* nearly all of them. *Car:* G-reg. Vauxhall Astra (metallic cat vomit colour). *Income:* £23,000

The ones that got away

On the following two pages are pictures of some of those whom I was unable to include.

1. Steve Jolley, unavailable. 2. Sandy Bullock, not found. 3. Paul Smith and Steve Lyle, not found. 4. David Lindgren, declined. 5. Niall Sweetnam, not found. 6. Keith Ball, declined. 7. Robin Knowles, declined. 8. Jo Winterbotham, declined. 9. Roger Hyams, unavailable. 10. Jonathan Obermeister, declined, according to his mother. 11. Suzanne Askham, declined. 12. Keith Turnbull, not found. 13. Unknown.

Louise Bell, who appears in the photograph on page 66, was unavailable.

1

2

3

4

5

6

7

8

9

10

11

12

13

Acknowledgements

Many thanks to Rachel Bell who has been an enormous help in tracing people, correcting my English and providing endless valuable editorial advice. Special thanks to her also for agreeing to be the first contemporary picture and allowing me to show her text so widely to the others who have participated.

Many thanks to Zelda Cheatle, for turning an idea from an amateur into an exhibition and a book; and to Peter Campbell for showing me that design really is an art. Many thanks also to Martin Reed of Silverprint; to Pamela Edwards for her untiring assistance; and to my wife, Anna Guggenheim, for spending many hours studying pictures of strangers.

With fond memories of Stein Falchenberg (1942 to 1995) of Teamwork Photographic who gave me his time and was kind enough to take me seriously.